Thanksgiving
TURKEYS

Thanksgiving
TURKEYS

Patrick Merrick

THE CHILD'S WORLD®, INC.

Library of Congress Cataloging-in-Publication Data
Merrick, Patrick.
Thanksgiving turkeys / by Patrick Merrick.
p.   cm.
Includes index.
Summary: Introduces the holiday of Thanksgiving and
some of the ways in which it is celebrated, explaining
the origin and meaning behind such symbols as the turkey.
ISBN 1-56766-642-6 (lib. reinforced : alk paper)
1. Thanksgiving Day—Juvenile literature.
2. Turkeys—Juvenile literature. 3. n–us n–cn.
[1. Thanksgiving Day. 2. Turkeys.]   I. Title.
GT4975.M47   1999
394.2649—dc21   98-50659
CIP
AC

Photo Credits

© Bill Aron/Tony Stone Images: 10
© 1991 Carl R. Sams, II/Dembinsky Photo Assoc. Inc.: cover, 23
© 1997 Carl R. Sams, II/Dembinsky Photo Assoc. Inc.: 30
© Christian Titlow/TRANSPARENCIES, INC.: 24
© Chuck Pefley/Tony Stone Images: 9
© 1999 Comstock, Inc.: 6
© Corbis/Bettmann: 19
© David Young-Wolff/Tony Stone Images: 13
© 1998 E.R. Degginger/Dembinsky Photo Assoc. Inc.: 26
© John Kelly/Tony Stone Images: 20
© Michael Quan/Tony Stone Images: 29
© Photri-Microstock: 16
© 1994 Ron Sherman: 15
© 1991 Sharon Cummings/Dembinsky Photo Assoc. Inc.: 2

On the cover...

Front cover: This wild turkey is showing its tail feathers to other turkeys.
Page 2: From up close, it is easy to see the beautiful colors on this turkey's body.

Table of Contents

What Is Thanksgiving?

Thanksgiving is a **holiday.** This means that it is a special day for people to be with their friends and family. On this day, people get together and remember all the things for which they are thankful.

In the United States, it is usually late fall before the farmers are completely done picking, or **harvesting,** their crops. Because of this, Thanksgiving is always held on the fourth Thursday of November. In Canada, harvest is earlier, so Thanksgiving Day is on the second Monday of October.

This farmer is harvesting his corn crop in the fall. ⇒

Many families have different **traditions,** or ways of doing things, when it comes to Thanksgiving. For some people, it is a time to visit churches and to pray. For others, it is a time to watch football and start thinking about Christmas shopping. For most people, it is a time to visit family and friends and to eat lots of food.

⇐ This family's tradition is to have a big meal with their loved ones.   11

As a way of showing how thankful they are, many people take time to **donate,** or give, their time and money to help people who are less fortunate than they are.

However, for almost everyone, the main part of Thanksgiving is the big meal that is prepared and eaten. For these people, the best part of the meal is the Thanksgiving Day turkey!

This family is enjoying the smell of the turkey before they carve it. ⇒

Do Many People Celebrate Thanksgiving?

Most parts of the world have special days for giving thanks. However, the United States was the first country to have an official Thanksgiving Day. We celebrate Thanksgiving as a way to remember what the first European settlers went through when they came to America.

This class is having a meal much like the first Thanksgiving. ⇒

The first Thanksgiving happened more than 370 years ago. Back then, a group of people called **Pilgrims** sailed from England over to North America because they wanted freedom. However, they were not ready for the harsh winter, and many of them died. The next spring, a Native American named *Squanto* helped the Pilgrims. He taught them how to find food. Because of his help, the Pilgrims had enough food to survive the next winter.

⇐ This picture shows some Pilgrims arriving in North America.

17

To celebrate, the Pilgrims held a huge three-day feast. During this time, they ate good food and played a lot of games. They also invited all the Native Americans who had helped them. While the Pilgrims did not call this celebration Thanksgiving, we now have Thanksgiving Day to honor those Pilgrims and Native Americans.

The first Thanksgiving might have looked like this artist's painting. ⇒

Because Thanksgiving started as a way to celebrate the fact that the Pilgrims had enough food, food has become a central part of the day. Most families have a big meal around the middle of the day. At this meal, you can find corn, sweet potatoes, bread, pumpkin pie, and other great food. However, the main dish is a big, brown, juicy, roasted turkey!

⇐ This table is full of Thanksgiving foods.

Why Do We Eat Turkey?

Turkey has been an important part of Thanksgiving since the days of the Pilgrims. The reason is that the turkey is a bird that is **native** to America. This means that it has always lived in this part of the world. So, when the Pilgrims started hunting for food here in North America, there were a lot of big wild turkeys. We eat turkey at Thanksgiving time because that is what was eaten at the first Thanksgiving.

This wild turkey is watching out for danger. ⇒

When the Pilgrims arrived, all the turkeys they found were *wild*. This means that the turkeys lived in the woods and were not raised on a farm. Wild turkeys used to live all over the eastern United States. In fact, the wild turkey was so popular that Benjamin Franklin wanted the turkey to be the national bird instead of the bald eagle!

⇐ This wild turkey lives in Arizona.

However, after hundreds of years of overhunting, wild turkeys were in danger of becoming **extinct.** When a kind of animal becomes extinct, there aren't any more of those animals left. Today, people have been trying to bring wild turkeys back. Now you can find wild turkeys in almost every state, and they are doing very well. However, most people do not eat wild turkeys—they eat farm turkeys instead.

← Farm turkeys like these are often much lighter in color than wild ones.

What Is a Farm Turkey?

A long time ago, people caught wild turkeys and instead of killing them for food right away, began to raise them on farms. Today, these farm turkeys do not look much like their wild cousins. They are much bigger, have different colors, and can't fly. These birds are raised on turkey farms throughout the United States.

Almost all of the farm turkeys sold today are bought to be eaten during the Thanksgiving and Christmas holiday season. How many turkeys is that? Almost 300 million turkeys are raised on farms every year!

This farm turkey was raised in the state of New York. ⇒

There are as many different recipes for Thanksgiving turkey as there are families who eat it. You can barbecue it, roast it, and make soup with it. You can put it in sandwiches, or even serve it on toast! No matter how you eat it, the turkey has become a **symbol** of Thanksgiving—something that reminds us of the day. It helps us remember the Pilgrims and all the things for which we are thankful. So, when you see or smell a Thanksgiving turkey cooking, take a moment to realize just how blessed you are.

⇐ This beautiful wild turkey has fanned out its tail feathers.

Glossary

donate (DOH–nayt)
When you donate something, you give it to someone else. Many people donate their time or money to make Thanksgiving nicer for people who are less fortunate.

extinct (ek–STINKT)
When a kind of animal becomes extinct, there aren't any more of those animals left. Wild turkeys were once in danger of becoming extinct.

harvesting (HAR–veh–sting)
When farmers harvest crops, they pick them. Most farmers harvest their crops in the fall.

holiday (HOL–lih–day)
A holiday is a special day that people celebrate every year. Thanksgiving is a holiday.

native (NAY–tiv)
A native is a person, animal, or plant that still lives in the place where it was born. Wild turkeys are native to North America.

Pilgrims (PILL–grimz)
The Pilgrims were the first people who left England to live in North America. The Pilgrims celebrated the first Thanksgiving.

symbol (SIM–bull)
A symbol is an object or word that is used to stand for something else. The turkey is a symbol of Thanksgiving.

traditions (tra–DIH–shuns)
Traditions are ways of doing things that are passed down from year to year. Eating turkey on Thanksgiving is a tradition.

Index